Esp

From

_____

Date

_____

Written and compiled by Tracy M. Sumner.

ISBN 978-1-60260-640-1

Published by Barbour Publishing, Inc., P.O. Box 719, Uhrichsville, Ohio 44683, www.barbourbooks.com

Our mission is to publish and distribute inspirational products offering exceptional value and biblical encouragement to the masses.

Member of the
Evangelical Christian
Publishers Association

Fun Facts for
FISHERMEN

BARBOUR
PUBLISHING

A recent U.S. Fish and Wildlife Service report estimates that recreational fishing is a popular pastime for nearly 60 million people in the United States.

Fishing is sometimes called "angling"—and people who fish are sometimes called "anglers"—because of the old English word angle, which was used centuries ago in reference to a fishhook or fishing tackle.

*Though not all of them are considered game fish,
there are more than 25,000 identified species of fish living on
earth. That's more species than all the amphibians, reptiles, birds,
and mammals combined. Some scientists believe there are
more than 15,000 fish species yet to be identified.*

Scientists have placed each species of fish into one of three large classes, or "superclasses." The largest class is the bony fishes, which includes most game fish. There are also cartilaginous fish, which have skeletons made of cartilage and not bone. Sharks and rays are cartilaginous fish. Finally, there are the jawless fish, which include species such as lampreys and hagfish.

Fishing with a rod has been traced back as far as the time of the Greek poet Homer, who lived in the ninth or eighth centuries BC. It is believed that the fishing line at that time was made either of horsehair or finely woven flax, and that the rod was made of Arundo donax, *a bamboolike plant native to the Mediterranean area.*

Time is but the stream I go a-fishing in.
Its thin current slides away, but eternity remains.

HENRY DAVID THOREAU

You can tell the age of many fish by taking a look at the "growth rings"—known as "circuli"—on their scales. The rings correspond to seasonal changes in the environment where the fish lives—very much like the rings in trees. The rings formed during the summer are usually farther apart, while the rings formed in the winter are closer together. Each pair of rings on the fish's scale indicates one year.

The state of Florida claims two popular game fishes as its state fish. In 1975 Florida's state legislature designated the Florida largemouth bass as its official state freshwater fish. That same year, the Atlantic sailfish was named the Sunshine State's official state saltwater fish.

There are four basic types of trout flies in popular use in the early twenty-first century: dry flies, wet flies, nymphs, and streamers. Dry flies imitate insects that float on the top of the water; wet flies are fished underwater and imitate insects, minnows, grubs, and other things trout eat; nymphs, which are often weighted, imitate the larval stage of aquatic insects; and streamers imitate minnows and other small fish.

GONE FISHING

*During the spawning period of some fish species
(for example, the largemouth bass), the urge to reproduce
overshadows other urges—even the urge to eat. After spawning,
the male largemouth guards his nest until the young are
free-swimming. During that time, he doesn't eat but will attack
other fish—as well as fishing lures—that happen by the nest.*

And God said, "Let the waters swarm with swarms of living creatures, and let birds fly above the earth across the expanse of the heavens." So God created the great sea creatures and every living creature that moves, with which the waters swarm, according to their kinds, and every winged bird according to its kind.

Genesis 1:20–21

*All fish species have certain characteristics in common.
All are cold-blooded, meaning their body temperatures adjust
to the temperature of the water they live in. All have gills that
collect oxygen from the water and put it into their bloodstreams.
All fish have fins (though some species have more and/or larger
fins than others). Most fish have scales that protect their
bodies from predators and other
dangers in the water.*

The blue marlin spawns in the late summer and fall. A single female can scatter more than 5 million eggs at once and can spawn several teams each spawning season.

The mako shark is a ferocious predator that can remain dangerous even after it is dead. Makos have been known to bite unsuspecting passersby even after they have appeared dead for several hours. One such incident took place several years ago at Ocean City, Maryland, where a tourist brushed the head of a dead mako lying on a dock.

The popular Australian game fish called the barramundi is an oddity in the fish world because nearly all barramundi are born male but then turn into females when they are three to four years old.

Of the estimated 60 million people who fish recreationally in the United States, about one in three fishes for largemouth bass, which is America's most popular game fish. The most popular saltwater game fish is the flounder.

There is certainly something in fishing that tends to produce a gentleness of spirit, a pure serenity of mind.

WASHINGTON IRVING

The American Heart Association recommends eating fish twice a week. That's because fish is a good source of protein, vitamins, and other important nutrients. Fish is also a great source of omega-3 fatty acids, which are essential to human health and which help prevent heart disease. Game fish such as mackerel, salmon, and tuna are high in omega-3 fatty acids.

The American Museum of Fly Fishing, which was established in 1968 in Manchester, Vermont, holds a collection of fly-fishing memorabilia and equipment that includes more than 1,200 fly rods, 400 reels, and 20,000 flies.

Chinook salmon migrate up to 4,000 miles from the ocean to the same freshwater spawning grounds where they were born. Once they arrive, the female lays thousands of eggs (sometimes more than 4,000) in a "redd," a nest she has dug to lay her eggs in, and the male salmon then fertilizes them with his sperm.
Both the male and female die within minutes of spawning.

Fish have all the senses humans have—touch, taste, sight, hearing, and smell. But they also have a sixth sense. Fishes' lateral lines, which are faintly visible and run down the fish's side from the gill covering to the tail, are made up of thousands of tiny hairlike cells that are sensitive to pressure waves and low-frequency vibrations.

Many people tend to think of recreational fishing as something the "guys" do. But an increasing number of American women have taken up fishing in recent years. According to statistics from the American Sportfishing Association (ASA), about 25 percent of all anglers in the United States are women.

On the Great Lakes, offshore winds have been known to create severe hazards for ice fishermen. The winds sometimes break off miles-wide sheets of ice, which strands large numbers of fishermen. That was the situation in February 2009, when local authorities and the Coast Guard had to rescue 100 stranded Lake Erie anglers.

Even though catch-and-release fishing has become increasingly popular, especially among fly-fishermen—not to mention a great way to preserve and protect fish populations—you'll never see an angler in Norway taking part in the practice. That's because activists in that country hold that it is unethical to perform any action that could be painful to a fish not kept for food. So if you catch a fish in Norway, you'd better be prepared to cook it!

The sailfish is not only one of the most beautiful game fish in the world, it is also the fastest swimming. Sailfish, which are found in the warmer sections of all the world's oceans and can weigh up to 200 pounds, have been clocked at speeds of over 68 miles per hour.

Who has ascended to heaven and come down? Who has gathered the wind in his fists? Who has wrapped up the waters in a garment? Who has established all the ends of the earth? What is his name, and what is his son's name? Surely you know!

PROVERBS 30:4

It's impossible to say just when recreational fly-fishing got its start. But the second/third-century Roman writer Claudius Aelianus described the practice of Macedonian fishermen, who ". . .planned a snare for the fish, and get the better of them by their fisherman's craft. . . They fasten red. . .wool round a hook, and fit on to the wool two feathers which grow under a cock's wattles, and which in colour are like wax. . . ."

If people concentrated on the really important things in life, there'd be a shortage of fishing poles.

DOUG LARSON

GONE FISHING

The largest freshwater fish ever hauled in with a rod and reel (bigger fish have been netted or speared) was a 468-pound white sturgeon caught in 1983 near Benicia, California, by Joey Pallota III of nearby Crocket, California.

According to the International Game Fish Association's (IGFA) list of world records, the biggest saltwater fish ever caught with a rod and reel was a 2,664-pound white shark. Alfred Dean of Irymple, Victoria, Australia, caught the fish on April 21, 1959. Amazingly enough, a year later, Dean also caught the second-largest fish on record, a white shark weighing 2,344 pounds. Dean also caught another great white weighing 2,536 pounds.

Salmon and steelhead, both of which are popular among fishermen who live near coastal areas of the United States, are examples of anadromous fish. Anadromous fish begin their lives in freshwater streams, migrate to the ocean to grow and mature, then return to the place they were born to spawn and begin the process over.

Largemouth bass, which are probably the most popular game fish in the United States, were originally found in the U.S. only east of the Mississippi River and south of the Great Lakes. But stocking programs have made it possible for anglers to catch largemouths throughout the continental U.S. as well as in Hawaii, southern Canada, and Mexico. Largemouth bass have also been stocked in Europe, Asia, Africa, and South America.

If you're the kind of angler who never keeps any of the fish you catch, you might consider using just flies and other artificial lures. Studies have shown that fish caught on natural bait (like worms or minnows) are far more likely to die after they are released than those caught on flies and lures. A third of all fish caught on natural bait will die after release, while nine out of ten caught on artificial lures survive.

GONE FISHING

For most people, fishing is a means of relaxation. But for fishermen after the wels catfish, which lives in Europe, fishing can become a life-and-death adventure. Wels catfish can reach ten feet in length and weigh 440 pounds. In July 2000, fisherman Anto Schwarz lost his life after hooking a huge wels catfish. While fighting the fish, Schwarz lost his balance and was dragged into the water, where he became entangled in his line and drowned.

Barometric pressure, changes in temperature, weather fronts, the position of the sun, and clouds are all weather factors that can affect the quality of fishing. Falling barometric pressure tends to influence fish to become more active along shorelines, which usually means better fishing. Rising pressure, on the other hand, causes a decrease in fish activity.

Experts on ice fishing—not to mention emergency personnel—recommend four inches of ice to walk on, five to six inches for snow machines and snowmobiles, seven to twelve inches for light cars, and fourteen to sixteen inches for full-sized trucks.

GONE FISHING

The two best times to fish is when it's rainin' and when it ain't.

PATRICK F. MCMANUS

The salmonfly, an important source of food for trout on many western U.S. streams and rivers, spends from two to four years of its life living in the water as a nymph. However, once it emerges from the water as an adult, it usually lives less than a week before mating and depositing its eggs in the water. During that mating period, trout often gorge themselves on the adult flies.

Five different species of salmon live on both sides of the Pacific Ocean and are considered Pacific salmon. They are the chinook (king), the sockeye (red), the coho (silver), the pink (humpback), and the chum (keta or dog) salmon. All of these fish die after spawning.

An estimated 50 million people enjoy fly-fishing worldwide. Most experts believe that number is growing and will continue to grow.

GONE FISHING

For his invisible attributes, namely, his eternal power and divine nature, have been clearly perceived, ever since the creation of the world, in the things that have been made.

Romans 1:20

Even though millions of anglers fish for largemouth bass every year, the world record for the species has stood for more than seventy-five years. In 1932, George Perry pulled the world record 22 pound, 4 ounce largemouth out of Georgia's Montgomery Lake.

A recent U.S. Fish and Wildlife Service report estimates that fishers generate more than $45 billion in retail sales and create a $125 billion impact on the U.S. economy. All this fishing—and spending money on fishing—creates work for more than one million people.

One out of every four freshwater fish, and one in every ten of all fish, is a catfish. As of 2007, 3,023 species of catfish have been identified. Many of these species are valued for food and for recreational fishing.

Fish don't grow like humans and other warm-blooded animals. Rather than reaching a certain size at maturity and then stopping, like we humans do, most fish continue to grow in length and weight until they die.

In my family, there was no clear division between religion and fly fishing.

NORMAN MACLEAN

The most expensive fishing lure ever made is fittingly called the Million Dollar Lure. Made by MacDaddy Fishing Lures of Shell Beach, California, it's a twelve-inch trolling lure—designed to catch marlin—made of three pounds of gold and platinum encrusted with 100 carats (exactly 4,753 stones) of diamonds and rubies. The price? One million dollars!

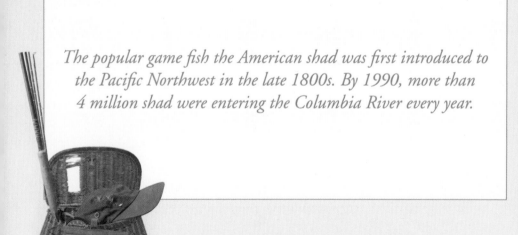

The popular game fish the American shad was first introduced to the Pacific Northwest in the late 1800s. By 1990, more than 4 million shad were entering the Columbia River every year.

In 1939, DuPont began marketing nylon monofilament fishing lines. The early monofilament lines didn't catch on with all fishermen because it was difficult to cast and handle. But in 1959, DuPont introduced Stren, which was thinner and much softer and could be used in many kinds of reels. This product caught on big-time with fishermen, and it remains popular to this day.

The peacock bass, a beautiful, ferocious, hard-fighting game fish in Brazil and in Florida, isn't a bass but a member of the cichlid family—the same family that includes popular aquarium fish such as oscars, freshwater angelfish, and Jack Dempseys. Larry Larsen, a well-known fisherman and author, calls them "freshwater bullies" due to their ability to damage or destroy even the stoutest fishing gear when they strike.

The surfperches, which include several species of game fish found off the shores of the Pacific coast in the United States, are unusual ocean fish in that they give birth to fully developed young rather than laying eggs.

One of the most popular artificial lures for largemouth bass is the plastic worm. These lures are sold in many different sizes and colors, but their effectiveness brings up the question: "Why do bass seem to like them so much?" Plastic worms don't really imitate anything largemouths usually eat, and even the most learned experts are stumped at why they work so well.

*Half of the starry flounder found along the coasts of Washington,
Oregon, and California are right-eyed (meaning the eyes
are the right side of the head), and half are left-eyed.
On the coast of Alaska, 70 percent of starry flounder are right-eyed.
But in Japan, all starry flounder are left-eyed.*

While it isn't known for sure how far back the use of fishhooks dates, archaeological finds have shown that metal fishhooks were used during Old Testament times. Also, bronze fishhooks have been found in the ruins of the ancient city of Pompeii, which was destroyed in 79 AD by an eruption by the volcano Mount Vesuvius.

There are seven known species of gar, the largest of which is the alligator gar, a fierce-looking freshwater fish that can grow to ten feet long and weigh more than 350 pounds. Despite its size and appearance, the alligator gar is harmless to people— though its eggs are poisonous to humans if eaten.

When I look at your heavens, the work of your fingers,
the moon and the stars, which you have set in place,
what is man that you are mindful of him,
and the son of man that you care for him?

PSALM 8:3–4

GONE FISHING

Bragging may not bring happiness, but no man having caught a large fish goes home through an alley.

UNKNOWN

There are two species of Pacific salmon that live only in the waters of Asia: the masu (also known as the yamame) and the amago (also known as the biwamasu) salmon.

The caviar considered the best in the world is imperial (golden ossetra) caviar or beluga caviar, which comes from sturgeon caught in the Caspian Sea. This caviar goes for as much as $500 an ounce, and prices are still rising due to the effects of pollution and overfishing of Caspian Sea sturgeon.

Bull sharks, which are popular as game fish, seem to like freshwater. These fish have been seen around 2,500 miles up the Amazon River in South America and have been caught around 900 miles up the Mississippi River. In Nicaragua, they have been seen leaping up river rapids—like a salmon jumps rapids and waterfalls to reach spawning grounds— to reach Lake Nicaragua.

Striped bass, also known to fishermen as stripers, is the state fish of Maryland, Rhode Island, and South Carolina. It is also the state saltwater fish of New York. Like salmon and steelhead, striped bass migrate from saltwater to freshwater to spawn.

Seven different species of tuna are caught both commercially and by sports fishermen. Those species are the albacore, the bigeye, the blackfin, the bluefin, the bonito, the skipjack, and the yellowfin. Yellowfin are the biggest U.S. commercial tuna catch, and the bluefin, which grows to over 1,000 pounds, is probably the most prized game fish of the tuna species.

Spey casting is a fly-fishing technique in which the angler uses a longer, heavier two-handed fly rod called a spey rod. This type of casting allows the angler to make longer casts and to avoid obstacles on the shore. It is used on large rivers for salmon, larger trout, and steelhead and also sometimes used in saltwater surf casting.

It is believed that the use of a fishing reel to hoist in fish has its origins in twelfth-century China. A painting dated around 1195 AD depicts an angler sitting on a raft using what many believe is the first handled reel. (It looked very little like what fishing reels look like now!)

In some situations, fishermen use flies or lures that make a lot of noise and stir the surface of the water. The reason? Most fish don't see especially well in the water but are very sensitive to sound and vibration. Simply put, some fish often hear their next meal before they see it.

GONE FISHING

Three-fourths of the Earth's surface is water, and one-fourth is land. It is quite clear that the good Lord intended us to spend triple the amount of time fishing as taking care of the lawn.

CHUCK CLARK

Ray Bergman's Trout, *is a classic book on fly-fishing. Written in 1938, it is the only fishing book to remain continuously in print for more than 50 years. When it was originally published, it contained more than 600 meticulously rendered flies, painted by the famed artist Dr. Edgar Burke.*

The sockeye salmon is a bluish-silver color during its adult life in the Pacific Ocean. But when it enters freshwaters to begin its journey to its spawning grounds, it turns bright red on the body and deep green on the head. Millions of sockeye make their way up British Columbia's Adams River every year to spawn, turning the entire river bright red and drawing crowds to watch from viewing platforms along the river.

All species of Pacific salmon die soon after they spawn, but steelhead—which are actually a type of sea-run rainbow trout—may travel from the ocean into freshwater to spawn several times over during their lifetimes.

The brown trout is one of the most widespread and popular game fish in the United States. But this species isn't native to U.S. waters; it was introduced into lakes, rivers, and streams here about 100 years ago.

I will open rivers on the bare heights,
and fountains in the midst of the valleys.
I will make the wilderness a pool of water,
and the dry land springs of water.

ISAIAH 41:18

The bluegill reproduces so freely that they are sometimes introduced to waters to serve as food for larger fishes, such as largemouth bass. Bluegills will overcrowd a pond or small body of water very quickly if they aren't thinned out by predators or fishermen.

Jack crevalle (or crevalle jack) is an aggressive, hard-fighting warm-water game fish found in the Gulf of Mexico and up the Atlantic coast of the United States. While they are prized as game fish, they aren't considered a good eating fish because they often carry ciguatera poisoning.

*The coho salmon, also known as the silver salmon, is native to the
Pacific Ocean but has been introduced to the Great Lakes,
where it is now a popular game fish for fishermen
on both sides of the U.S./Canada border.*

There will be days when the fishing is better than one's most optimistic forecast, others when it is far worse. Either is a gain over just staying home.

RODERICK HAIG-BROWN

A great way to get young children started fishing is to take them to ponds where panfish such as crappie, perch, rock bass, bluegill, sunfish, and pumpkinseeds can be caught. These small fish usually aren't finicky when it comes to the bait they'll take, and they don't grow large enough to make it difficult for the kids to reel them in.

GONE FISHING

The ferocious, high-jumping shortfin mako, a close relative of the great white shark, is one of the most acrobatic, athletic fighters any game fisherman can hope to hook up with. These fish, which can grow as large as 1,000 pounds, have been known to jump as high as twenty feet out of the water when hooked— higher than a blue marlin. Hooked makos have been known to attack fishing boats!

*Contrary to what you might have seen in the movies,
the red piranha, which is native to the Amazon River basin,
will not attack and kill people who happen to swim too close to
them. Piranhas will occasionally nip at swimmers, and they
are known as a nuisance to fishermen in the area. But they
are an excellent eating fish that will take a
variety of live baits and artificial lures.*

The green sturgeon is one of the most migratory species of sturgeon known. Some green sturgeon caught and tagged in the Sacramento/ San Joaquin estuary have been caught a year later in the Columbia River and Grays Harbor, Washington.

Both white crappie and black crappie are attracted to lights at night. That makes these fish excellent targets for night fishermen who set up lanterns on shore to attract the fish. The best baits for crappie are small minnows and jigs.

Barracudas—warmwater predator fish with huge, sharp teeth—don't attack people. In fact, barracudas actually tend to shy away from people. They have, however, been known to lurk around fishing boats and attack hooked fish.

Lake trout, which are also called mackinaw, isn't technically a trout but a char. The lake trout is the largest of all chars, weighing up to 100 pounds. In 1961 a 102-pound lake trout was gillnetted in Lake Athabasca, Saskatchewan. These fish also live very long lives. Larger fish are 20–25 years old, and some specimens reach 40 years of age.

The females of the Pacific halibut species live far longer and grow far bigger than the males. Females live up to 42 years and grow up to around 105 inches long, while the males live about 27 years and grow to 54 inches. So if you catch a "barn door" halibut (meaning a really big one), it's most likely a female.

Oscars are popular aquarium fish that some hobbyists say will become extremely tame and learn to recognize their owners. But they've also become a popular game fish in Florida, where they have escaped from flooded fish farm ponds or aquariums and begun breeding in the wild. Sports fishermen say oscars fight better than bass and that they are an excellent eating fish.

According to a report by the American Sportfishing Association (ASA), Florida leads the United States in the number of anglers, at about 2.77 million, and in the number of jobs supported by recreational fishing at 75,100. Texas is second in both categories, with about 2.52 million anglers helping to create about 59,000 jobs.

For "the earth is the Lord's, and the fullness thereof."

1 CORINTHIANS 10:26

Often, I have been exhausted on trout streams, uncomfortable,
wet, cold, briar scarred, sunburned, mosquito-bitten.
But never, with a fly rod in my hand, have I been in
a place that was less than beautiful.

<small>CHARLES KURALT</small>

People who fish for pacu—a large game fish found in South America—use some very strange bait, including small fruits, seeds, and nuts. Even though a pacu has a mouthful of large teeth and powerful jaws, it eats mostly nuts and fruits it gathers near the surface. Theodore Roosevelt wrote of catching and eating pacu in his book Through the Brazilian Wilderness.

American author Zane Grey was an avid big-game fisherman who spent a lot of his time fishing for sharks, marlin, and other billfish during his visits to Australia and New Zealand. He also helped establish deep-sea sport fishing in New South Wales, Australia, and wrote of his fishing experiences in his book An American Angler in Australia.

GONE FISHING

The International Game Fish Association (IGFA) world record for a rainbow trout caught on a rod and reel is 43 pounds, 6 ounces, caught on June 5, 2007, by Adam Conrad on Lake Diefenbaker in Saskatchewan. But the all-time largest rainbow (not caught on rod and reel) was a 57-pound behemoth estimated to be eleven years old.

You probably learned early that a dolphin, even though it swims in the ocean, is a mammal and not a fish. But one popular game fish—the mahi-mahi—also goes by the name "dolphin" or "dolphin-fish." Mahi-mahi are found in the Caribbean Sea, in the Gulf of Mexico, on the west coast of North America and South America, on the Pacific coast of Costa Rica, and in many other places worldwide.

*Before the arrival of the settlers to the Pacific Northwest,
an estimated ten to sixteen million salmon and steelhead
made their way from the Pacific Ocean into the rivers
of the Columbia River basin to spawn every year.
Today, fewer than 1.5 million fish return every year.*

Fishermen can be the superstitious types. For instance, one superstition shared by many professional bass anglers is that it's bad luck to have a banana on the boat. One pro bass angler, Gerald Swindle, discovered that his partner had brought a banana on his boat. Swindle was so upset at the fruit's presence that he immediately returned to the dock and made his partner get rid of it.

GONE FISHING

Adult swordfish have no scales or teeth.
They swallow their food whole.

One of the biggest differences between Atlantic salmon and Pacific salmon is that some Atlantic salmon survive after spawning and can actually spawn again, while all *Pacific salmon die after spawning. Also, there is only one species of Atlantic salmon (salmo salar), while there are several species of Pacific salmon.*

The first mention of a dry fly (a fly fished on top of the water) in print was on December 17, 1853, in a periodical called The Field. *In an article by a writer identifying himself as "The Hampshire Fly Fisher," he states, "On the other hand, as far as fly fishing is concerned, fishing upstream, unless you are trying the Carshalton dodge and fishing with a dry fly, is very awkward."*

*The great charm of fly-fishing is that we are always learning;
no matter how long we have been at it, we are constantly
making some fresh discovery, picking up some new wrinkle.
If we become conceited through great success, some day
the trout will take us down a peg.*

THEODORE GORDON

Izaac Walton (1593–1683) is best known as author of
The Compleat Angler *(1653), one of the three most published
books in English literature (the other two are the Bible and
the* Complete Works of Shakespeare*). The Compleat Angler
has been printed in more than 300 editions.*

Archaeological finds have shown that the ancient Egyptians were fishing with rods, lines, and hooks by the year 2000 BC. The early Egyptian hooks were made of copper, and had no barbs. The hooks' heads were made by doubling the end of the shank over.

The landlocked salmon, which has been called the king of freshwater fish, is a subspecies of the Atlantic salmon that lives in several lakes in the eastern part of North America. Landlocked salmon spawn between mid-October and late November in streams and rivers between the lakes they live in. These fish are nonmigratory, even when they have access to the ocean.

GONE FISHING

You visit the earth and water it;
you greatly enrich it; the river of
God is full of water. . . .

PSALM 65:9

Even though dry flies are among the bestselling for trout, these fish find the majority of their food under water. Trout feed 75 percent of the time or more on nymphs and smaller fish near the bottom, but they are opportunistic feeders that will feed on readily available insects such as mayflies, stone flies, and caddis flies.

The red drum—also known as the redfish, red bass, spottail, and channel bass—gets its name from the strange drumming sound the male makes during mating season. As the male makes this sound, he nudges the female to get her to lay her eggs, which he then fertilizes.

Minnesota is known as the land of 10,000 lakes, but, depending on how you define a lake, there may be more than 15,000 lakes there. These "lakes" range in size from less than one-third of an acre all the way up to Lake Superior, the largest of the Great Lakes. Many of these lakes have populations of trout, walleye, crappie, pike, and muskellunge, so it's no wonder that fishing is popular year-round in Minnesota.

GONE FISHING

The kokanee, a popular—and tasty—game fish found in lakes and reservoirs throughout the northern part of the United States, is actually a landlocked form of the sockeye salmon. Kokanee are usually much smaller than the regular sockeye, measuring 10–18 inches and weighing 2 or 3 pounds as compared with the sockeye, which can measure up to 33 inches and weigh 4–8 pounds.

The Bassmaster Classic, which is considered one of the biggest (if not the biggest) fishing competitions in the world, got its start in 1971 in Lake Mead, Nevada. Since that time, the tournament has grown into a three-day spectacle covered extensively by the sports network ESPN. Fifty-five of the world's best pro bass fishermen compete in the event. First-place prize money has grown from $10,000 in 1971 to $500,000 as of 2006.

To more fully enjoy fly-fishing, the angler needs the right "line weight" of rod. Here is a quick look at the line weights and which fish they are best for:

Weight 1–3: *Small trout and panfish.*

Weight 4: *Small to medium (up to 15 inches) fish.*

Weight 5–6: *Trout and smaller bass.*

Weight 7–8: *Large trout and large bass.*

Weight 9–14: *Saltwater fish and salmon and steelhead.*

Nothing makes a fish bigger than almost being caught.

UNKNOWN

*According to the United States Fish and Wildlife Service,
the Paiute cutthroat trout is the rarest trout in the U.S. and possibly
in the world. This fish is found only in a nine-mile stretch of
Silver King Creek in Alpine County, California.*

The meat from wild salmon gets its orange/pink color from the krill (small, shrimplike crustaceans) salmon eat while they are in the ocean. Because farmed salmon don't have krill in their diets, pigment is added to their meat to make it look like that of the wild fish.

The marlin uses its bill, which is actually an extension of its upper jaw, to slash at schools of the fish it eats to kill or stun them. Marlins also use their bills for protection.

Which of the fifty states would you guess had the most miles of rivers?
California and Texas both seem like good guesses, and so does
Alaska. But, believe it or not, Nebraska has more miles
of rivers than any other state in the United States.

Weiss Lake, a 32,000-acre freshwater lake located near Cedar Bluff, Alabama, is known as the Crappie Capital of the World and is host to many local, state, and national crappie fishing tournaments.

A recent National Oceanic and Atmospheric Administration (NOAA) fisheries survey held that recreational saltwater fishing in the United States generated $82 billion in sales, $24 billion in income, and supported 534,000 jobs in 2006.

The earliest known fishing rods looked nothing like the rods anglers use today. They were made of wood, bone, or stone (later they were made of metal) and were called gorges. They were only about an inch long and pointed at both ends. Fishermen attached bait and line to the gorges and fished from boats. It wasn't long before anglers used longer rods made of tree branches.

He makes me lie down in green pastures.
He leads me beside still waters.
He restores my soul.

PSALM 23:2–3

It has always been my private conviction that any man who pits his intelligence against a fish and loses has it coming.

JOHN STEINBECK

*While there is debate about how fish actually perceive color,
most agree that fish can see shades, reflected light, and shapes.
Still, most fishermen know that certain colors of lures and flies
work better than others when it comes to catching fish.*

Statistics from the United States Fish and Wildlife Service show that since 1955, the total number of people who enjoy recreational fishing has more than doubled and has increased a rate much greater than the growth in general population.

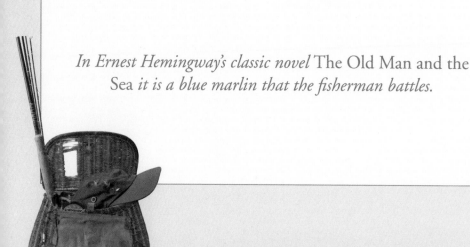

In Ernest Hemingway's classic novel The Old Man and the Sea *it is a blue marlin that the fisherman battles.*

GONE FISHING

The roosterfish, a popular saltwater game fish common around Mexico, Costa Rica, and Panama, as well as in the eastern Pacific waters from California to Peru, is distinguished by a strange-looking dorsal fin with seven long spines that make it look like a rooster's comb.

Baudette, Minnesota; Garrison, Minnesota; Isle, Minnesota; Ray, Minnesota; Rush City, Minnesota; Garrison, North Dakota; Mobridge, South Dakota; Port Clinton, Ohio; Shell Lake, Wisconsin; and Umatilla, Oregon all claim the title of "Walleye Capital of the World."

Some fishermen believe the bonefish, which is found in shallow, warm saltwater such as the Florida Keys, may be pound-for-pound the strongest, fastest game fish in the world. When hooked, a bonefish can strip 100 yards of line of the fisherman's reel in a matter of seconds.

The game fish American fishermen refer to as walleye or walleyed pike is mostly known in Canada as pickerel, jackfish, or dore. Although the walleye is sometimes called walleyed pike, it is actually a member of the perch family.

Game fish are too valuable to be caught only once.

LEE WULFF

GONE FISHING

The largemouth bass and the smallmouth bass are the best-known of the game fish called "black bass." Other types of black bass are the spotted bass, the shoal bass, the redeye bass, the Suwannee bass, the Guadalupe bass, and Bartram's Bass. Scientists don't consider any of these species true bass but members of the sunfish family.

The oldest-known preserved fly in existence is one tied in the year 1789—the same year George Washington was inaugurated. The fly is on display at the American Museum of Fly Fishing in Manchester, Vermont.

All the romance of trout fishing exists in the mind of the angler and is in no way shared by the fish.

HAROLD F. BLAISDELL

In January 2001, a high-quality 444-pound bluefin tuna sold in a Japanese fish market for a world record $173,600.

In early November of 2003, Tracey Shirey, a South Carolina construction worker, paid more than $100,000 for a 10-inch copper Haskell Minnow, a fishing lure made by Riley Haskell of Painesville, Ohio in the 1850s. Shirey outbid seven other bidders for the collector's item at the Lang's Sporting Collectibles' fall auction.

For thus says the LORD, who created the heavens (he is God!),
who formed the earth and made it (he established it;
he did not create it empty, he formed it to be inhabited!).

ISAIAH 45:18

After spending the first one to eighteen months in freshwater as fry and smolts, chinook salmon spend one to eight years at sea maturing before returning to the stream where they began their lives to spawn and then die.

The saltwater game fish known as the cobia is not only a strong fighting and excellent eating fish, it is also one of the most migratory saltwater fishes known. Cobia winter in the Gulf of Mexico then migrate as far as Maryland for the summer.

GONE FISHING

Some studies have shown that more than 75 percent of all coho and chinook salmon caught in Pacific Northwest fisheries began their lives in hatcheries rather than in the wild.
The number is even higher for steelhead. . .88 percent.

The longest-standing official International Game Fish Association world record is for the yellow perch. On May 1, 1865—almost a century and a half ago—Dr. C. C. Abbot caught a four-pound, three-ounce yellow perch out of a lake near Bordentown, New Jersey, that still stands as a world record for any freshwater species.

According to an obscure law, all sturgeon caught in British waters are technically property of the Queen. However, the last time a sturgeon was eaten at Buckingham Palace was reportedly in 1969. England is home to one native sturgeon species, although it is believed to be close to extinction.

Next to prayer, fishing is the most personal relationship of man.

HERBERT HOOVER

The white sturgeon is not only the largest freshwater fish in North America—reaching lengths of more than 20 feet and weights of more than 1,500 pounds—it is also the longest-living fish in the world. These fish can live for more than 100 years, and some specimens are believed to have reached 150 years old.

The Arctic grayling, which looks something like a salmon/trout hybrid with a huge dorsal fin, likes cold water. . .really cold water. Grayling thrive in the ice-cold waters draining into the Pacific and Arctic oceans in Canada, Alaska, and Siberia.

The Apache trout is one of just two species of fish to be native to a single state. This fish is native to Arizona only, and is also known as the Arizona trout. It is also Arizona's official state fish.

While running for president, Dwight D. Eisenhower tried—quite unsuccessfully—to teach his running mate, Richard Nixon, to fly-fish. "It was a disaster," Nixon later confessed. "After hooking a limb the first three times, I caught my shirt on the fourth try. The lessons ended abruptly."

During a single spawning, the female largemouth bass produces around 5,000 eggs. Of those, only about 10 will reach any level of maturity. One reason for the low survival rate is that the parents often eat their own young in feeding frenzies. That after the male largemouth fiercely protects the eggs and, for a short time, the hatchlings!

The Mongolian taimen, a popular game fish—especially for fly anglers—native to a large area in Eastern Europe, is the biggest member of the salmonid trout family. The International Game Fish Association record is a little under 100 pounds, but a taimen caught in 1988 weighed in at 231 pounds.

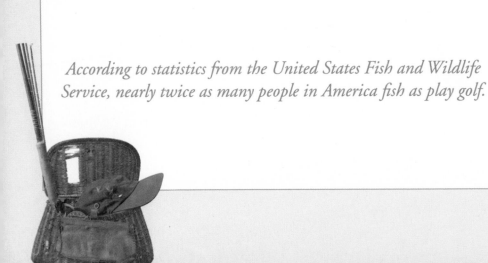

According to statistics from the United States Fish and Wildlife Service, nearly twice as many people in America fish as play golf.

*Many go fishing all their lives without knowing
that it is not fish they are after.*

HENRY DAVID THOREAU

Come and see what God has done:
he is awesome in his deeds toward the children of man.

PSALM 66:5

The spotted sea trout—also known as sea trout, speckled trout, spotted weakfish, or black trout—is not really a trout at all. It is actually closely related to the red drum, another popular game fish.

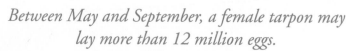

Between May and September, a female tarpon may lay more than 12 million eggs.

With a surface area of 31,700 square miles (not to mention a maximum depth of 1,332 feet), Lake Superior is the world's largest freshwater lake. Lake Superior is known for excellent salmon and trout fishing. Fishermen catch chinook, coho, and pink salmon in Lake Superior as well as rainbow trout, brown trout, steelhead, and lake trout. Walleye and smallmouth bass are also caught there.

Many flatfish—including flounder, halibut, and sole—are popular both as game fishes and as table fare. The eyes of adult flatfishes are usually on one side of their heads—the side facing up from the bottom—but they aren't born that way. Newly hatched baby flatfish have an eye on each side of their heads, just like most other fish, but as they mature one eye migrates to the other side of the head.

The name of the game fish Dolly Varden comes from a popular dress from the 1870s. The story goes that it was suggested by a woman who encountered some fishermen who were admiring a large, colorful trout one of them had landed. When the woman, who was wearing her Dolly Varden dress, heard that the anglers wanted to give the fish a better name, she suggested, "Dolly Varden," because it reminded her of her colorful, new dress.

Bonefish feed on what is called "benthic" marine life, which refers to animals that live on the ocean floor. Fishermen have witnessed bonefish following manta rays and stingrays so they can feed on the worms, young fish, shrimp, small crabs, and other creatures the rays stir up from the sand when they swim by.

The swim bladder—which most fish carry in their body cavities and which is usually filled with oxygen—is the organ that helps fish swim upright and which allows them to swim at their depth without floating upward or sinking downward. In some fish species, the swim bladder is filled with oil instead of oxygen.

The fishing was good; it was the catching that was bad.

A. K. BEST

The Australian salmon, also known as the Australasian salmon and as the kahawai in New Zealand, isn't related to the salmon family of fishes at all. This fish got its name from European settlers who saw that it somewhat resembled the salmon they had seen in Europe. Australian salmon, which are a saltwater fish, are popular game fish in Australia and New Zealand.

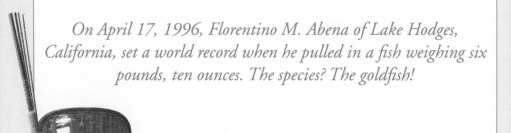

On April 17, 1996, Florentino M. Abena of Lake Hodges, California, set a world record when he pulled in a fish weighing six pounds, ten ounces. The species? The goldfish!

Isinglass is an almost pure gelatin prepared by cleaning and drying the air bladders of sturgeon, cod, hake, and other game fishes. It is used as a clarifying agent for wines and beers and as a glue and/or cement. Isinglass is produced in the United States, Canada, Brazil, Russia, the West Indies, and the Philippines.

GONE FISHING

The tiger trout, which gets its name from its tiger-stripe markings, is a sterile hybrid of the brown trout and the brook trout that has been widely stocked for recreational fishing. Tiger trout are produced in hatcheries by fertilizing brown trout eggs with brook trout milt and then heat shocking them. This process creates an extra set of chromosomes and increases the survival rate of the eggs from 5 percent to 95 percent.

The zander—also known as the pike perch—is a popular game fish in Europe. One weekend in July of 2009, a 17-plus pound zander made news when it attacked six swimmers in southern Switzerland's Lake Maggiore. After unsuccessfully attempting to net the fish, police divers harpooned and killed the zander, which was then cooked up and served up to tourists at the lake.

The snook, a hard-fighting game fish found in the warm coastal waters of the western Atlantic Ocean and the Caribbean Sea, is a master at using several tools to its advantage when it is hooked. If the snook's razor-sharp jaws don't cut through the angler's line, then the fish is quite adept at using shoreline roots and mangroves to aid in its escape.

GONE FISHING

Praise the LORD from the earth,
you great sea creatures and all deeps,
fire and hail, snow and mist,
stormy wind fulfilling his word!

PSALM 148:7–8

In 2005, British golf pro Gary Hagues caught a world record 83-pound, 8-ounce mirror carp from France's Rainbow Lake. After getting an official weight recorded for the fish, Hagues tagged it and released it. A year later, Hagues returned to the same lake, and, amazingly enough, caught the same fish. The carp had gained some weight, giving Hagues a new world record of 87 pounds, 2 ounces.

In 2007, the Bassmasters competition included competition for women for the first time. They competed in a separate event, on February 8–10 at Lake Amistad in Del Rio, Texas. The winner of the event was Juanita Robinson of Highlands, Texas.

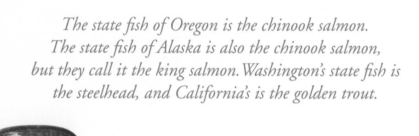

The state fish of Oregon is the chinook salmon.
The state fish of Alaska is also the chinook salmon,
but they call it the king salmon. Washington's state fish is
the steelhead, and California's is the golden trout.

Some go to church and think about fishing,
others go fishing and think about God.

TONY BLAKE

Fishing with dry flies—ones that float on top of the water and imitate adult insects—didn't become popular with fly anglers until the second half of the twentieth century. In fact, by the year 1900, hundreds of wet fly patterns were in use, but very few, if any, dry flies really caught anglers' attention.

The author of the first English book on recreational fishing was a woman named Juliana Berners, whose Treatyse of Fysshynge wyth an Angle *was first published in 1496. Her book, which was reprinted several times during the sixteenth century, included information on the construction of fishing rods, on the use of natural bait and artificial lures, and on angler etiquette.*

The International Game Fish Association (IGFA) Hall of Fame and Museum in Dania Beach, Florida, includes an extensive collection of sports fishing information, exhibits, educational classes, fishing demonstrations, interactive displays, and virtual reality fishing. Also on display are 170 species of world record game fish, along with information plates displaying the date the fish was caught, the name of the angler, and where it was caught.

An alligator gar, a game fish species found in the lower Mississippi River Valley and southeastern United States, can survive up to two hours out of water after it has been caught.

Birchwood, Wisconsin, is the bluegill capital of the world.
Watchapreague, Virginia, is the flounder capital of the world.
Fort Thompson, South Dakota, is the paddlefish capital of the world.
And Okeechobee, Florida, is the speckled perch capital of the world.

On July 25, 2009, William Ludwick of Ortonville, Minnesota, established a fly-fishing world record when he landed a 51-inch, 50-pound muskellunge using a nine foot, 10-weight fly rod. The giant fish took Ludwick's homemade twelve-inch streamer fly.

Up until the mid-1800s, bass fishermen usually relied on live baits such as minnows and crawfish. Around that time, however, the first artificial lures for bass were developed. These lures were actually variations of trout and salmon flies. In time, flies specifically designed for bass were introduced, as were spinner/fly lures. Around 1900, floating wooden lures called plugs appeared on the scene.

In July 2005 Thai fishermen netted what is believed to be the world's largest catfish, a 646-pound Mekong giant catfish. Had the monster fish been caught on a rod and reel, it would have easily surpassed the International Game Fishing Association world record for largest freshwater fish ever caught, a 468-pound sturgeon.

Tenkara fishing is one of the most popular methods of angling among fly-fishers in Japan. This type of fishing is used mostly for small-stream trout. In tenkara fishing, the angler uses only a rod, a tenkara line, and fly; no reel is used. Tenkara fly rods are long— between twelve and fifteen feet. The use of the long rod allows the fisherman to more precisely place his fly on small pools.

I don't know exactly what fly fishing teaches us,
but I think it's something we need to know.

JOHN GIERACH

By faith we understand that the universe was created by the word of God, so that what is seen was not made out of things that are visible.

HEBREWS 11:3

Before synthetic materials such as fiberglass and graphite became widely available, many fishing rods were made from split Tonkin bamboo, which was light yet strong and flexible. Even today, many fly-fishermen still use Tonkin split-bamboo rods and consider them the finest available.

The Big Blackfoot River, a snow-fed and spring-fed river in western Montana, is the stream featured in the 1976 Norman Maclean novella A River Runs Through It *as well as the 1992 film based on Maclean's story. The Big Blackfoot is renowned for its fly-fishing.*

Franklin Delano Roosevelt, the thirty-ninth president of the United States, was an avid fisherman whose physical disability due to polio didn't stop him from enjoying the pastime. FDR had specially-rigged chairs installed in his fishing boats, which allowed him to enjoy fishing.

In today's bass fishing competitions, every effort is made to make sure that the fish caught are released unharmed. The bass are placed in a well-oxygenated live well and released as soon as they are weighed by tournament officials. Fish that appear overly stressed are sometimes placed in tanks and treated before they are released. Also, anglers are heavily penalized for bringing dead fish to weigh-in.

*A fourth-century BC written account from China
describes fishing with a bamboo rod, silk line,
and needle used as a hook,
and rice as bait.*

Every January, Gull Lake, located north of Brainerd, Minnesota, hosts what is billed as the world's largest ice-fishing contest. More than 10,000 anglers show up every year, and more than 20,000 holes are drilled in the ice.

The grayling belongs to a genus of fish called Thymallus, *which is part of the family salmonidae (the salmon family). The genus name refers to the aroma of wild thyme the fish's flesh gives off when it is fresh.*

Chester Arthur, the twenty-first president of the United States (1881–85), was an avid fisherman before and after he entered the White House. It is believed that his love of fishing helped increase the popularity of the sport during that time in our nation's history. "There was nothing I loved more than fishing for salmon," Arthur once said.

The first known New World reference to fly-fishing was from 1766 and appears in the diary of English scholar Joseph Banks.

There he stands, draped in more equipment than a telephone lineman, trying to outwit an organism with a brain no bigger than a breadcrumb, and getting licked in the process.

PAUL O'NEIL

He said to them, "Follow me,
and I will make you fishers of men."

MATTHEW 4:19